Documenting History

Documenting the Industrial Revolution

Peter Hicks

rosen publishing's
**rosen
central**

New York

Published in 2010 by The Rosen Publishing Group Inc.
29 East 21st Street, New York, NY 10010

First Edition

Senior editor: Camilla Lloyd
Designer: Phipps Design
Consultant: Dr. Andrew Dilley
Picture researcher: Shelley Noronha
Indexer and proofreader: Cath Senker

Library of Congress Cataloging-in-Publication Data

Hicks, Peter, 1952–
 Documenting the Industrial Revolution / Peter Hicks.
    p. cm. -- (Documenting history)
 Includes bibliographical references and index.
 ISBN 978-1-4358-9670-3 (library binding)
 ISBN 978-1-4358-9677-2 (paperback)
 ISBN 978-1-4358-9678-9 (6-pack)
 1. Industrial revolution--Great Britain--History. 2. Industrial revolution--History. I. Title.
 HC254.5.H53 2010
 330.941'081--dc22
                                      2009025862

Photo Credits:
The author and publisher would like to thank the following for allowing their pictures to be
reproduced in this publication: Cover: Main: Bettman/CORBIS, BL: Wolvertonhampton History
& Heritage Society, BR: Wayland Picture Library; 1 Wayland Picture Library, 5 Mary Evans
Picture Library, 6 Science Museum/Science & Society Picture Library, 8 Wolvertonhampton
History & Heritage Society, 9 Guildhall Library, City of London,The Bridgeman Art Library,
10 Public Record Office/HIP/Topfoto, 11 courtesy of the Ironbridge Gorge Museum
Trust(www.ironbridge.org.uk <http://www.ironbridge.org.uk/>), 12 James Watt ©
Bettmann/CORBIS, 13 Wayland Picture Library, 14 Science Museum/Science & Society Picture
Library, 15 Peter Hicks, 16 Science Museum, London, U.K. /The Bridgeman Art Library, 17, 18
Peter Hicks, 19 Peter Newark American Collection/The Bridgeman Art Collection, 20 Mary
Evans Picture Library, 21 Musee D'Orsay, Paris, France, Giraudon/The Bridgeman Art Library,
22 Peter Hicks, 23 Mary Evans Picture Library, 24 Wayland Picture Library, 25 National
Railroad Museum/Science and Society Picture Library, 27 Nationalgalerie, SMPK, Berlin,
Germany/The Bridgeman Art Library, 28 Mary Evans Picture Library, 29 Science
Museum/Science & Society Picture Library, 30 Currier and Ives/Getty Images, 32 Peter
Newark American Pictures/The Bridgeman Art Library, 33 Peter Newark American
Pictures/The Bridgeman Art Library, 34 Archives Charmet/The Bridgeman Art Library,
35 Akg-Images, 36 Mary Evans Picture Library, 37 Mary Evans Picture Library, 39 ©
Bettmann/CORBIS, 40 Guildhall Library, City of London/The Bridgeman Art Library, 41
Collection Kharbine-Tapabor, Paris, France/The Bridgeman Art Library, 42 Mary Evans
Picture Library, 43 Hulton Archive/ Getty Images, 44 © Bettmann/CORBIS.

Manufactured in China
CPSIA Compliance Information: Batch #WAW0102YA: For Further Information
contact Rosen Publishing, New York, New York at 1-800-237-9932

CONTENTS

CHAPTER 1
BRITAIN: THE FIRST INDUSTRIAL NATION 4

CHAPTER 2
STEAM, COAL, AND IRON 12

CHAPTER 3
THE FACTORY SYSTEM 18

CHAPTER 4
THE TRANSPORTATION REVOLUTION 22

CHAPTER 5
INDUSTRIALIZATION SPREADS 26

CHAPTER 6
STEAM AND TRANSPORTATION 32

CHAPTER 7
URBANIZATION AND THE SOCIAL COSTS 36

CHAPTER 8
PROGRESS AND PROBLEMS 40

TIMELINE 45

GLOSSARY 46

FURTHER INFORMATION AND WEB SITES 47

INDEX 48

What was the Industrial Revolution?

The word *revolution* means great change or upheaval. The upheaval that happened over many years in Britain during the eighteenth and nineteenth centuries was so remarkable that by 1851, Britain had become known as "the workshop of the world." Britain changed from a rural country, dependent on the land and agriculture for its wealth, to the world's first industrial nation, where goods were manufactured in factories. These goods were sold at home and abroad, encouraging trade and making the country wealthy. The Industrial Revolution that began in eighteenth-century Britain spread to Europe and the U.S.A. and changed the world.

Until around 1780, most Britons lived and worked on the land, growing crops and rearing animals. Britain was a regional country, meaning that people lived and worked in their home villages or towns. Travel was very difficult because roads in most places were poor and transportation was expensive, slow, and uncomfortable. Each region had its own city or market town (where food and animals could be bought and sold) and a port allowing goods to be imported and exported by sea and river.

The population was small. In 1750, it was roughly 6 million and only one-fifth of people lived in towns. Over the next 100 years, the population tripled to 20 million and by 1851, over half the people lived in towns and cities. Britain had transformed into an urban nation.

Britain did not depend only on agriculture before the industrial revolution. There were industries, too—iron and textiles—but they were small scale. Woolen cloth was used for clothing, and this was spun and weaved in people's cottages, often involving the whole family. This manual production was called the domestic system, because it was centered on the home.

SOURCE

BOOK

"By all the processes being carried on under a man's roof, he retained his individual respectability; he was kept apart from associations that might injure his moral worth, whilst he generally earned wages which were sufficient to live comfortably upon …"

Peter Gaskell pointed out the advantages of the domestic system.

Peter Gaskell: extract from *The Manufacturing Population of England*, published in 1823.

Spinning on the green in Colchester, England. The scene in the painting looks idyllic, the domestic system was flexible, and families could work when they had to.

Traveling merchants would deliver raw wool by packhorse and take away the woven cloth (yarn). Women spun the thread on their spinning wheels and men wove the cloth from the threads on their hand looms. There were shortages of thread because the invention of John Kay's "flying shuttle" in 1733 had sped up the weaving process and allowed the weaver to produce wider cloth, which meant that weaving was much faster than spinning. In one day, a weaver would use up the thread that had taken a spinner all week to produce.

Britain's small iron industry was also undeveloped. Although there were large deposits of iron ore in Britain, there was a serious lack of fuel to smelt it. Until the early eighteenth century, charcoal was used as the main fuel, but the woodlands providing the trees for the charcoal were being used up. Some iron was imported instead from Sweden, Germany, and Russia, where there were huge wood reserves.

The rapid population growth between 1700 and 1900 changed Britain and quickened the transition from manual production at home to machine production in factories. Britain's industrial changes aroused interest in Europe and the United States. It would not remain the workshop of the world for very long

The importance of population and agriculture

During the eighteenth century, agriculture went through a revolution that transformed the look of the British countryside. The cause of this change was primarily population growth. From 1700 to 1800, Britain's population increased by 3.5 million to about 10 million. There were many more mouths to feed and this put huge demands on food production. As demand increased, the price of food went up. This in turn created an incentive for enterprising farmers to make healthy profits from their land.

To achieve this, farmers had to modernize their traditional systems of agriculture. The open-field system that dated from the Middle Ages, with its small strips of land dotted around a village, could produce enough food when the population was small. When the population increased dramatically, this old system could not deal with the change. The old system was not very efficient. For instance, at any one time, one-third of the land was fallow—it was not farmed in order to allow the soil to regain its nutrients.

SOURCE

BOOK

"...by nineteen out of twenty enclosure bills, the poor are injured, and some grossly injured."

The agricultural writer, Arthur Young, admitted that enclosure caused a great deal of hardship to many.

Arthur Young in *Reformation to Industrial Revolution* by Christopher Hill, 1967.

A model of S. Morton's seed drill, 1828. The drill sowed seeds at an even rate per yard and could be adjusted to vary the depth, according to the farmer's requirements.

Rich farmers bought up many of the strips of land and enclosed them into larger fields. To do this, farmers had to get an Enclosure Act passed through Parliament (part of the British government). Since Parliament at that time represented landowners, this was easily passed. Nearly 5,000 acts were passed between 1761 and 1800.

Once the bigger farmers put ditches and hedges in the fields on their neat farms, they could improve the soil and experiment with new crops, animal breeds, and machinery.

A new four-year crop rotation replaced the old and wasteful three-year cycle of wheat, barley, and fallow. Farmers now planted wheat, turnips, barley (or oats), and clover. This put land under cultivation all the time, with the turnips and clover replacing nitrogen in the soil.

Under the old system, animals often became ill by mixing together on the common land. The new hedged fields allowed for the introduction of new breeds of stronger, heavier animals.

Previously, seed was scattered onto the soil in the "broadcast" method and this was very wasteful. New machines, such as the seed drill, increased the yields of crops while using less seed. With the revolution in agriculture underway, people received a more plentiful, varied diet. Unsurprisingly, this helped the population to increase as it became healthier. An increase in population was important for two

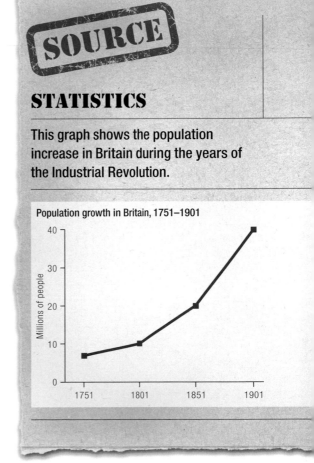

SOURCE

STATISTICS

This graph shows the population increase in Britain during the years of the Industrial Revolution.

Population growth in Britain, 1751–1901

reasons. First, there was a bigger workforce to work in the mills, factories, and workshops. Second, this workforce would have to buy goods and services such as clothes, shoes, housing, and food. This demand gave a huge boost to industry and agriculture.

Another result of the agricultural revolution was the drift of people from the countryside to the towns. Small farmers sold their strips of land and after spending the money they had made, tried their luck in the new and expanding towns and cities.

Paying for the Industrial Revolution

In the late eighteenth century, Britain was booming. A whole infrastructure of roads, canals, mills, docks, and warehouses was created. Where did all the money to pay for this come from? A great deal of the funding came from abroad. Britain was building up an empire and colonies such as India were very valuable. The East India Company pioneered trade in India, especially in textiles, and fortunes were made, much of it returning to Britain.

During this time, slaves from Africa were bought with British exports and then traded in the Caribbean and the U.S.A. in return for raw materials. Huge profits were amassed from the slave trade. Enormous personal fortunes were made from slavery by businessmen dealing in ships, tobacco, cotton, sugar, and rum. Much of these profits were then poured into economic ventures at home. The slave trade relied on selling goods, often cotton imported from India. This market was one that industrialists were later able to exploit. The ports of Bristol and Liverpool engaged in the slave trade and were then able to invest in new docks and warehouses.

SOURCE

SHARE CERTIFICATE

The share certificate is for one share in the Darlaston Steel and Iron Company Limited. Richard Bills formed the company in 1826 and by the 1850s, the site of the furnaces and foundry covered over 55 acres (22 hectares). The company employed about 2,000 people, and when Bills' stepson retired, it was sold to the Lloyd family for £250,000 (around $27.6 million today). This share certificate is from October 1875.

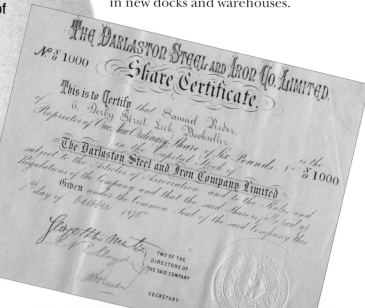

The Bank of England, Threadneedle Street, London. Founded in 1694, it looked after the government's accounts and provided loans in peace and wartime.

Some money came into Britain from other nations such as the Netherlands, which saw Britain as a safe and profitable country in which to invest. However, a huge amount of the investment for the Industrial Revolution came from British landowners and farmers at home, who were making substantial profits from their modern farms and estates. They placed their savings in the hundreds of new banks that sprang up after 1780. These banks would then lend money to businessmen starting new enterprises, such as cotton production. By 1800, there was a huge amount of money in circulation. There were 400 private banks around the country—often based in market towns—and 70 banks in London alone.

These banks did not only provide loans, but also allowed bills to be paid. Banks started introducing checks, which allowed businessmen to settle transactions without having to move large amounts of cash around. If someone had an idea for a new business project, they did not have to go to a bank for a loan. They could form a company and issue shares in it. If people bought shares, they became shareholders in the company. If the company was a success, they would receive a share of the profits.

An example of such a project was the Ironbridge—the world's first bridge made of iron—built across the River Severn near Coalbrookdale in Shropshire. To pay for it, the company issued 64 shares at £50 (around $6,000 today) each. This was a very high price at that time. When all the shares were sold, the money paid for the design, materials, and labor to build the bridge. It opened in 1781, and users were charged a toll (fee) to cross it. From these tolls, the shareholders received a share of the profits. Many enjoyed a good return on their initial investment.

The importance of inventions and entrepreneurs

Another reason the Industrial Revolution happened first in Britain was the appearance of important inventions at critical times. We have seen that the speed of spinning lagged behind that of weaving. In 1765, James Hargreave's Spinning Jenny (named after his wife) was the first step in the advance in spinning. The first machine made in Blackburn, Lancashire, had eight spindles harnessed to a hand treadle (a lever used to turn a wheel). As the machines developed further, the number of spindles increased to 80. By 1788, there were 20,000 machines in operation (small ones in cottages and large ones in factories). A disadvantage of the jenny was that although it spun good weft (the cross thread), it did not spin good warp (the long thread).

SOURCE

DRAWING

This is the patent design of Arkwright's Spinning Jenny in 1769.

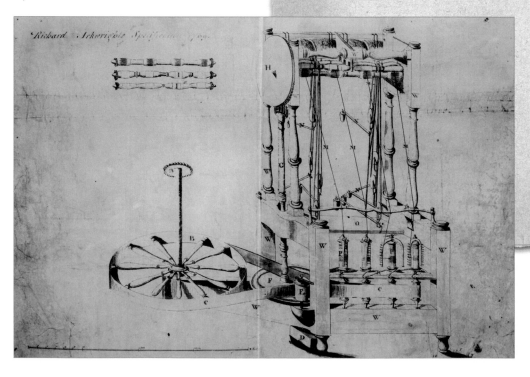

This particular problem was solved by Richard Arkwright, from Preston, Lancashire, one of the great pioneer businessmen of the Industrial Revolution. The machine he invented was the Water Frame, consisting of rollers and spindles that stretched the thread and made it strong enough or both warp and weft. As its name suggests, it was powered by water and not suitable for use in the home. In 1771, Arkwright built a factory to produce cotton cloth in Cromford, Derbyshire, powered by the fast-flowing river Derwent.

Arkwright was a dynamic entrepreneur, or "risk taker," who was constantly looking to make money by providing people with goods they wanted. When unemployed and disgruntled spinners burned down one of his mills, he simply opened another one. He died in 1782, one of the richest men in Britain.

One disadvantage of the Water Frame was that the yarn produced was strong but coarse. This meant the yarn could not be made into high-quality cotton fabric. Samuel Crompton, a weaver from Bolton, Lancashire, devised a machine that produced yarn that was strong and fine. In 1779, he crossed the Spinning Jenny with the Water Frame, creating a machine known as the Mule (a mule is a cross between a donkey and a horse). When it was perfected, spinning was revolutionized and by 1812,

William Reynolds was a businessman and an inventor who built a canal network linking his ironworks, mines, and factories in Shropshire. Two of his canals were on different levels, so he built a huge lift (Britain's first inclined plane) at Ketley Bank to raise the barges between them.

Mules drove millions of spindles across northern Britain. The textile industry was based in large factories, powered by fast-flowing rivers and streams. Richard Arkwright was one of many entrepreneurs who prospered during these years. Successful entrepreneurs understood that new goods needed to be in demand. They also realized that a knowledge of science and technology would benefit them. They understood the importance of investment and that cheap transportation of raw materials and finished products was crucial

Steam

Before the Industrial Revolution, wind, horses, and water provided power. These sources were unreliable—the wind did not always blow, in the summer, rivers and streams could dry up, and horse power was expensive. There was always a demand for power so people started experimenting to find a source of power that was constant, cheap, and not dependent on the weather.

The breakthrough came from solving the problem of flooding in tin, copper, and coal mines. Thomas Savery, a military engineer from Cornwall,

James Watt in his laboratory working on a model of a Newcomen engine. It was after he successfully repaired it that he improved the engine's design.

where there were many tin mines, developed his so-called "Miner's Friend" in 1698. It was a pump designed to raise water from flooded mines, but proved to be too slow and expensive.

Ten years later, Thomas Newcomen, a locksmith from Dartmouth in Devon, developed the first successful fire-driven machine. It consisted of a cylinder pushing up a piston attached to a crossbeam. When the steam drove up the piston, cold water was sprayed into the cylinder to make it drop down again. At the other end of the beam, a rod pumped water from the mine. Again, this engine was very expensive because the cooling system used so much fuel. Also its action, a beam

moving up and down, meant that it could pump up and down but couldn't turn a wheel. This limited what the engine could do. However, by the mid-eighteenth century, it still proved popular in mines all over the country.

Two important developments were to make steam engines more attractive. In 1764, James Watt, a brilliant maker of scientific instruments, repaired a Newcomen engine. In doing so, he radically improved its performance by overcoming its weaknesses. Instead of cooling the hot cylinder, Watt designed the cooling to take place in a separate condenser connected to the cylinder. The condenser could be kept cool while the cylinder was hot. Huge savings on fuel were made. Watt patented his engine with a separate condenser in 1769. Cheap and efficient steam power was now a possibility.

Later in 1781, Watt discovered that if he attached a rod to the crossbeam and placed a small cog rotating around a bigger one—the "Sun and Planet" gears—it could drive wheels. This rotary motion could power the new spinning machines in the cotton mills that were previously powered by water. The engines were also used in ironworks, coal and tin mines, on canals for raising barges, and pumping water and in breweries, brick works, and china factories. With more and more steam engines in use, there was a massive demand for coal. Industries

ENGINE PLAN

This plan shows James Watt's double-action Sun and Planet gears engine drawn in 1788.

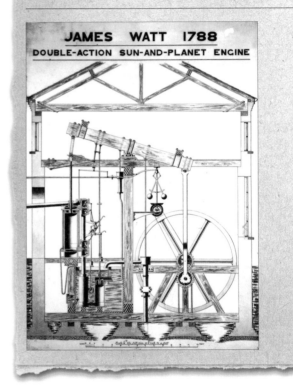

sprung up on and near the coalfields of the Midlands and northern Britain, Scotland, and South Wales, so they could be near the fuel that powered the engines. James Watt's partner, the entrepreneur Matthew Boulton, who helped build 1,200 Boulton and Watt engines by 1800, boasted; "*I sell, sir, what all the world desires—power.*"

The importance of coal

In the early eighteenth century, the coal industry was undeveloped and produced only 2 million tons a year. Much of this was used as domestic fuel, although some was exported to Europe. Most of this coal was mined near Newcastle and transported by ships mainly to London and ports along the south and east coasts.

The coal industry was small scale because mining technology was still primitive. Coal was mined when it was near the surface. Mining deeper seams was dangerous and expensive. Flooding was a serious problem, and so, too, were poor ventilation and potential explosions and cave-ins. Another difficulty was getting the coal to the surface.

SOURCE

PARLIAMENTARY PAPERS

"The youngest children in the mines ... are called ... trappers ... it is a most ... dull dungeonlike life these little creatures are doomed to spend; a life, for the most part, passed in the solitude, damp. and darkness."

Extract from *Children's Employment Commission (Mines), Parliamentary Papers*, 1842, Vol. XVI.

Pit explosions were depressingly common in the eighteenth and nineteenth centuries. Thousands of mine workers were killed in explosions before the compulsory inspection of pits was introduced in 1850. At first, seven inspectors were responsible for the safety of 3,000 mines.

With the increasing popularity of steam engines, there was a huge demand for coal as fuel. Mine owners were encouraged to dig deeper and bigger mines. This led to a build up of poisonous and explosive gases, making safe ventilation essential. Miners had their own names for these killer gases. Carbonic acid gas was named "blackdamp." It couldn't be seen but a telltale sign of its presence was when a miner's candle was put out. Methane gas is highly explosive and was known as "firedamp." This was visible and it was said it *"lay like snow in a drift."*

The early system of ventilation consisted of digging shafts on different levels, which allowed air to be drawn from one and up the other. To increase the air flow, a furnace was placed at the bottom of the up-shaft of the mine, drawing more clean air in. By the early nineteenth century, pumps were being used and ventilation slowly improved, but the death rate from explosions was high.

A big threat came from explosions caused by the use of naked flames in the pit. There were only two possible forms of lighting—candles and steel spark mills—and both could be lethal. The Davy Lamp and the Stephenson Lamp were invented in 1816. These lamps encouraged pit owners to send miners into even deeper and more dangerous places. In 1866, 651 miners were killed in firedamp explosions. Owing to the huge demand for coal,

The strip of wire gauze around the Davy Lamp that surrounded the flame conducted away its heat and prevented it from lighting any gas present.

there was a shortage of labor in the mines. Women and children were employed in shocking conditions. Women carried baskets of coal up flights of steps to the surface. Young girls pulled trucks of coal with chain ropes around their waists.

In this haphazard way, coal production increased. In 1770, 6 million tons were produced, rising to 10 million in 1800. By 1820, this doubled to an impressive 20 million tons. It was not just steam engines that consumed vast amounts of coal. The iron industry also started to demand coal after Abraham Darby, an iron master, discovered a way of smelting (extracting the metal from its ore) iron ore by using coal.

The iron masters

Britain's wood supplies for smelting iron ore were running so low that many iron masters tried to find a replacement for charcoal. They experimented with coal, but the impurities in it produced brittle and unworkable iron.

In 1709, Abraham Darby found that by reducing coal to coke—the sulfur was burned away—he could smelt the iron ore into good pig iron, which was brittle but good for casting into cannons, pillars, and pots. Coke-smelted pig iron could not be heated and beaten into wrought iron because it crumbled when hammered. The use of coke spread very slowly—it was a Darby family secret until the 1750s—and in 1760, there were only 17 coke furnaces in the whole of Britain.

It was said that Abraham Darby II first converted coke-produced pig iron into wrought iron, but he didn't leave any records. The man who patented it in 1784 was Henry Cort, working at Fontly Forge in Hampshire. He smelted the iron ore in a special furnace that used coal. The heat from the coal was reflected onto the iron ore by a specially angled furnace roof so

SOURCE

PAINTING

This dramatic painting by P. J. de Loutherbourg (1808) shows the powerful iron furnaces of Coalbrookdale, Shropshire, blasting out fire and heat.

that impurities did not spoil the iron. When the iron became molten, it was "puddled," or stirred with iron hooks, which allowed the carbon to burn off, leaving iron that could be shaped. In fact, Cort had invented a "rolling-mill." The metal passed between grooved rollers, making bars of iron. It was much quicker than the old method of heating and hammering by hand. Darby had improved the speed of pig iron production and Cort had perfected the turning of it into wrought iron. All this required coal, which Britain had in plentiful supply. Britain was entering a new "iron age."

Perhaps the greatest iron master of the age was John Wilkinson, nicknamed "Iron Mad" Wilkinson. Based in Birmingham, though he had works in Coalbrookdale, his father had been one of the first iron ore smelters to adopt Darby's coke method. He

The Ironbridge in Shropshire, England. The world's first iron bridge, it was completed in 1779 for £3,000 ($360,000 today). The bridge used 378 tons of cast iron.

himself had been an early purchaser of a Boulton-Watt steam engine. The iron output was enormous. His ironworks helped to build the world's first iron bridge near Coalbrookdale in association with Abraham Darby III.

Wilkinson provided the city of Paris with 40 miles of iron pipes for its water system. In 1787, he successfully launched the first river barge on the River Severn made from an iron plate. When Britain fought Napoleon in Spain—the Peninsular War (1808–14)—most of the cannons were made by Wilkinson. It was his skill in casting cannons that allowed engineers like James Watt to produce precise cylinders in their steam engines. Wilkinson died in 1808 and was buried in an iron coffin.

How factories worked

The new water—and later steam-driven mills—or factories that were built in the later eighteenth century were much more efficient than the old domestic system of industry. The machines and workforce were all in one place and everybody inside the factory buildings had a particular job to do.

In his book *The Wealth of Nations* (1776), the Scottish economist, Adam Smith, showed how a greater "*increase in the quantity of work*" resulted from the "*division of labor.*" He then showed how 16 different operations and

A cotton mill in full operation. Note the young girl cleaning the machinery while it is still moving. Mills like this were extremely noisy, hot, dusty, and dangerous.

workers could successfully manufacture pins. This division of labor was applied to the cotton industry.

The cotton mills had many floors with employees working on one part of the production process. In the Lancashire mills, this involved washing the raw cotton first, then carding (combing) it into strands ready to spin them on the water frames or mules into yarn ready for weaving. The jobs in these processes were varied. Reelers, winders, and frame cleaners all required different skills. Children were employed to change the bobbins and mend snapped threads.

Power looms were not in full use until the 1830s, so the weaving—especially for fancy cloths—was still performed by hand-loom weavers. With so much work, the weavers were in great demand and it was said you could tell a weaver in a northern town *"by the £5 notes in his hatband."*

Power was transmitted to all floors and processes by a series of gears, shafts, and belts connected to either a water wheel or steam engine. The factory buildings themselves had to be strong to cope with the weight of the machines and their continual violent motions. The first mills were made of wood and stone, but after a series of disastrous fires, cast iron columns, beams, and joists replaced wood in the 1790s.

Cotton production was centered on Lancashire for a number of important reasons. The soft water and damp climate helped the spinning. The presence of the Lancashire coalfields assisted expansion when steam power replaced water. Vast amounts of raw cotton grown on the slave plantations in the southern United States were imported through the port of Liverpool. The volume of exports increased after the development of Eli Whitney's "cotton gin" (short for

ENGRAVING

The cotton gin, invented by Eli Whitney in 1793, increased the demand for slaves in cotton production. This engraving shows their part in the process.

"engine") in 1793. First, circular saws removed the fiber from the seeds and then the fiber was removed by a revolving brush. This significantly sped up the process. In 1792, the U.S.A. exported 295 bales of cotton rising to 36,000 bales in 1800. By the 1840s, 85 percent of cotton spun in British mills came from the southern United States. There was a constant demand for cotton clothing by the working class in the nineteenth century, because it was cheap, light, and easy to wash.

Working conditions

In time, the new machines that transformed cotton production would spread to the woolen industry. Yorkshire woolen production prospered because the mills were close to coalfields, which provided an accessible supply of fuel. For this reason, the East Anglia and Somerset woolen industries went into decline. By the early nineteenth century, there were over half a million people working in the textile industry. What were conditions like?

The workers found the discipline of factory life very hard. Time keeping was vital. Clocks, bells, and whistles dictated their shifts—the amount of time they had to work. This was a world away from the old domestic system under which people worked when they needed to.

The mills were noisy, dusty, unbearably hot in the summer, and lit by gas lamps in the winter. Many machine operators worked very long

Campaigners such as Richard Oastler were very concerned about the treatment of children in mills and factories. He likened their conditions to those of the slaves in the Deep South.

FACTORY FINES

Any spinner found with his window open—1 shilling ($6 today)
Any spinner found washing himself—1 shilling ($6 today)
Any spinner putting his gas out too soon—1 shilling ($6 today)
Any spinner found whistling—1 shilling ($6 today)
Any spinner five minutes late after the last bell rings—2 shillings ($12 today)
The factory fines above were just some of the harsh rules enforced in many mills. If spinners broke the rules they had to pay the fines from their wages.

Fines from William Cobbett's *Political Register, Vol. II,* November 20, 1824.

shifts, often 15 to 16 hours a day. A combination of the long hours and early starts (5 or 6 in the morning) led to tiredness and accidents. There were many examples of workers dragged into unfenced machinery by their clothes or hair causing dreadful mutilation.

The men in charge of the machines—"overseers"—were very strict and workers could be fined for breaking the rules. If a spinner arrived five minutes after the shift bell rang, he or she was fined 2 shillings (10p or $12 in today's money). This was a serious deduction from a weekly wage of 50 pence–£1 (around $25–$50 today).

The work was hardest for the large numbers of children employed in the factories. These noisy places scared and bewildered the very young. Small children were popular with factory owners because they were cheap to employ and could clean the machinery while it was still running.

Why did parents allow their children to do this dangerous and tiring work? Many parents were poor and needed more money to come into the home. Other children were orphans sent from workhouses and orphanages to work as apprentices in the factories. Some of these children were treated very badly.

Not all factory owners were cruel. Robert Owen's New Lanark mill in upper Clydesdale, Scotland, provided a model village, school, places of worship, and good working conditions for his workers. Men did not work more than ten and a half hours a day and children under the age of ten did not work.

Metal workers in a foundry, 1893. Owing to unpleasant conditions—intense heat, smoke, and the dangers of molten iron—injuries were common.

Manufacturing did not just take place in the cotton and woolen mills of the Midlands and northern Britain. The Industrial Revolution created demand for a whole range of products that were produced in workshops (small factories), forges, brickyards, and sweatshops in all the big towns and cities. Men, women, and children toiled in overcrowded, poorly ventilated, and often harmful conditions to produce the iron, ropes, bricks, nails, chains, and glass that industrialization demanded.

Roads and canals

Britain would never have been able to industrialize without a revolution in transportation. We know Britain was very regional before the 1780s, and if industry and business were to thrive, communications needed to improve.

At the start of the eighteenth century, roads in Britain were poor. Little better than tracks, they became impassable in the winter. River transportation was limited because in the summer, water levels dropped so low that rivers were hard for barges and ships to navigate.

After the 1750s, roads started to improve because of the Turnpike Trusts. A Trust consisted of businessmen who raised money and got permission through an Act of Parliament to build or improve a road. Then they charged travelers tolls to use it. Tollhouses with gates were built at ends of the road, and the toll money was used to maintain the road and improve other roads.

The Trusts employed great road engineers such as Thomas Telford (1757–1834), whose London to Holyhead road contained the spectacular suspension bridge that linked Wales with the island of Anglesey. John McAdam (1756–1836) perfected a raised, cambered (curved) road surface made of layers of stone, with drainage ditches on either side. The weight of the traffic compressed the stones to form a "macadam" surface.

The turnpike network improved journey times—mail and ideas traveled quickly—and business communications improved. In the mid-eighteenth century, a horse-drawn coach journey between Edinburgh and London took between 8 and 10 days. By 1836, this

TABLE OF TOLLS

This was a list of the toll payments required to cross the Ironbridge in Shropshire.

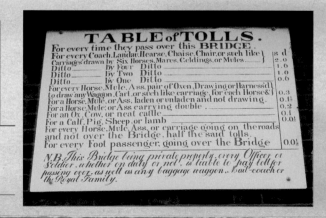

had been reduced to roughly 45 hours. Mail coaches began in 1784 and by 1800, almost 400 towns were getting daily mail delivered by coaches that could travel an average of 6 miles per hour (10 kph). However, industrial processes involved bulky goods—coal or iron ore—and sending these goods by road was difficult and expensive.

The Duke of Bridgewater, a coal mine owner in Worsley, found that the cost of sending his coal by packhorse to

MAP

This is a map showing the route of a proposed canal from Worsley to Manchester and then to the Mersey by the engineer James Brindley for the Duke of Bridgewater.

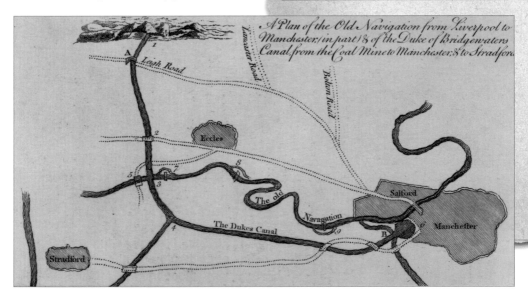

Manchester, 8 miles (13 km) away, was unprofitable. He decided to build a canal instead and hired a millwright, James Brindley, to design it. In 1759 and 1760, Parliament passed the acts allowing construction to begin. The impressive canal contained an aqueduct over the River Irwell and two tunnels, one of which had a water-driven crane that lifted the tubs of coal up a vertical shaft to the surface. The

construction nearly bankrupted the duke, but with an income of £3 million (ca. $360 million today) a year, he soon got his investment back. The Grand Trunk Canal, linking the rivers Trent and Mersey, opened in 1777 and traveled through five tunnels and over five aqueducts. Over the next 70 years, a 4,000-mile (6,440-km) network of canals was made, linking the coalfields, industrial towns, and important rivers.

Railway Mania

Although the canals helped to revolutionize transportation in the early nineteenth century, they were still not perfect forms of transit. Journey times were slow because of the many locks that barges had to go through when canals climbed hills. Canal docks became very congested, and goods could be held up for many weeks. Gradually, canal owners increased their prices, so businessmen were anxious to try alternative methods of carriage.

The railroad, or "tramway" to use its original name, was an old idea and had been used in mines and quarries where animals pulled wagons full of coal or stone. Some engineers experimented with steam locomotion. In 1805, Richard Trevithick's Catch Me Who Can entertained paying passengers on a circular demonstration track in

The excited spectators follow and cheer Stephenson's Locomotion at the opening of the Stockton to Darlington railroad in 1825.

London. The attraction proved popular but businessmen were uninterested in investing in it.

In 1812, William Hedley, a manager of a colliery in Northumberland designed the Puffing Billy, another early steam locomotive. However, it was George Stephenson, a colliery engine maker—known later as the "father of the railways"—who made an impression on the owners of the proposed Stockton to Darlington railroad.

On September 27, 1825, Stephenson's engine Locomotion, pulling wagons loaded with coal and flour (and about 600 people), arrived in Stockton. The railroad age had begun. Stephenson and his son Robert designed the Rocket that opened the Liverpool and Manchester railroad in September 1830. The businessmen who had the foresight to invest in this project saved £20,000 ($2,385,000 today) in transportation costs in six months. Railroads could make money out of carrying goods and passengers.

There followed a period of expansion called Railway Mania. The success of the Stockton to Darlington and Liverpool to Manchester railroads encouraged others to invest in the railroads. There was money in Britain ready to be invested that had come from other successes of the Industrial

Revolution, such as the textile industry. By 1851, nearly 7,000 miles (11,260 km) of track had been laid, and it took over from the canal network in linking up the major centers of population, business, and industry in Britain.

A huge army of navigators ("navvies") had built, largely by hand, an impressive infrastructure of cuttings, embankments, bridges, tunnels, and viaducts that carried the tracks. Their achievement, which cost the lives of many navvies, can be seen today. Railroad construction boosted British industries. There was huge demand for iron, coal, bricks, timber, gravel, and steam engines.

The railroads created a boom in Britain. People were employed to build and run them. The speedy transit of raw materials and goods brought down costs and opened up new markets. Farmers, for instance, could send their perishable produce (such as milk) to nearby cities by train, improving their income and the population's diet.

RAILROAD MAP

This is George Bradshaw's map of the British railroad network in 1851. Bradshaw was originally a map maker for canals and railroads. In 1839, he began to publish railroad timetables.

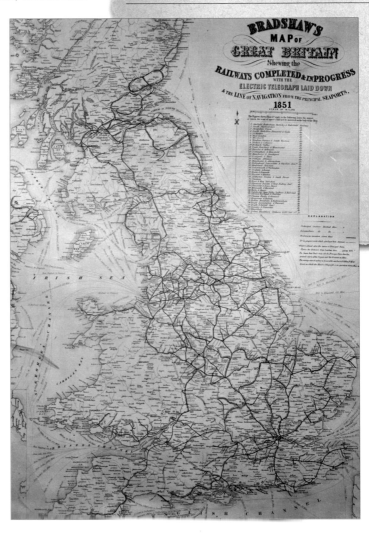

Europe follows Britain

Britain's success as the world's first industrial nation aroused the interest of its neighbors in Europe. Numerous groups of businessmen visited Britain in the 1820s and 1830s and were undoubtedly impressed by the mills, factories, forges, and mines that were powered by the smoke-belching steam engines. Many, it must be said, were also horrified by the filth, squalor, and pollution they noticed in the industrial areas and where the workers lived.

Spurred on by Britain's lead and the desire to modernize and make money, the Industrial Revolution spread east and south across Europe after 1820. The pace of change was not the same in every country. In some areas, towns that were on or near a coalfield changed and developed quickly. Northern France and the Ruhr valley in Germany adopted new mining and metalworking techniques quickly. Other parts of France, where there were huge timber reserves, were still using charcoal to smelt iron ore. In fact, as late as 1848, half of France's iron still came from charcoal furnaces.

Some countries with good reserves of raw materials lacked transportation structures. This is why Russia and Germany had to invest in railroads first to allow industrialization to follow. British locomotives were used in these country's early railroads.

After Britain, the next country to industrialize was France in about 1820, but slow population growth held it back. Germany started the process in 1840 and was an established industrial power by 1900, leading the world in some branches of chemical production, notably synthetic dyestuffs. Sweden, with huge reserves of iron ore, began industrializing in 1850. Austria, Italy,

SOURCE

BOOK

"A sort of black smoke covers the city. The sun seen through it is a disk without rays. Under this half-daylight, 300,000 human beings are ceaselessly at work. A thousand noises disturb this dark, damp labyrinth, but they are not at all the ordinary sounds one hears in great cities."

Alexis de Tocqueville was a French political thinker. He was shocked by what he saw in the city of Manchester when he traveled there in the nineteenth century.

Alexis de Tocqueville in *Journeys from England and Ireland*, 1835.

A German ironworks in Berlin, 1875. Metalworking was crucially important to Germany's industrialization. In 1850, it employed 12 percent of the manufacturing workforce. Fifty years later, this had risen to 27 percent.

and northern Spain began the process in 1870, and Russia the latest, in 1890. Russia, although potentially very powerful, was hampered by a lack of finance to invest in industry. By 1914, nearly half of Russia's capital for industry had come from abroad. Most of Europe was undergoing some measure of industrial transformation in 1900, exception for the Balkans.

Another factor determining the pace of industrialization was political stability. Some countries were very stable in the nineteenth century, others less so. Between 1789 and 1871, France went through four revolutions and lost two major wars. Russia was involved in two unsuccessful wars against Britain and France in 1854 and Japan in 1904–5. It also experienced a serious revolution in 1905. Germany, on the other hand, became a united

country after Prussia (the most powerful German state) waged two successful wars against Austria in 1866 and France in 1870–71. Germany's success in these wars boosted industry.

Britain was fortunate that there were no massive political upheavals at home in the nineteenth century. It was evolving into a reasonably stable democracy. After its success in the Napoleonic wars, which led to an increase in iron production, Britain did not fight another war in Europe until World War I in 1914. There is no doubt that Britain's industrial success inspired business leaders and governments across Europe to copy developments in textiles, coal mining, and heavy industry.

The United States industrializes

In 1800, the United States was a modest agricultural country; 83 percent of its workforce worked on the land. Its population was only 4 to 5 million. Over the next 60 years, the U.S.A. was to undergo a dramatic transformation. Its population rose to 30 million and the number of people living in towns and cities tripled. In 1860, the U.S.A. had 9 cities with over 100,000 people in each (Britain had 7). The New York–Brooklyn conurbation exceeded a million inhabitants and the city of Philadelphia, half a million. This represented a huge market for home-produced goods. The expansion came about because the northern United States underwent its own revolution in industry.

How did this revolution start? As in Britain, textiles were very important. Many countries looked to Britain for technology and expertise. The U.S.A. was no exception, and merchants from New England sent a group to Britain to recruit skilled workers. The British government responded by passing a law forbidding new plans, machines, and skilled labor from leaving the country.

However, in 1789, Samuel Slater (1768–1835), the manager of a Lancashire mill, secretly emigrated to the U.S.A. with the plans of all the

Robert Fulton's **Clermont** *on the Hudson River between New York and Albany. The "Watt-type" engine burned pine wood and was described as a* "monster moving on the waters ... breathing flames and smoke."

The "father of American industry," Samuel Slater. His expertise and extraordinary drive gave the U.S. textile industry a huge boost.

own. By 1800, 2,000 spindles were working, but by 1815, stimulated by the war against Britain in 1812, there were 130,000 spindles operating in more than 200 mills. When Slater died in 1835 (a very rich man), he had set up mills in Rhode Island, Massachusetts, New Hampshire, and Connecticut.

By 1825, the U.K. parliament had lifted the export ban. Many textile workers were encouraged to move to the U.S.A. with their machines and know-how. Lowell, a town in Massachusetts, was founded at this time by Boston merchants on the Merrimac River, a good source of power for the new mills. It was soon a thriving settlement, and power looms for weaving were introduced, based on the latest British designs. Similar towns were founded along the Merrimac and in southern Maine.

U.S. engineers did not always get their ideas from abroad. From the 1790s, many inventions were successfully developed at home. In 1795, Oliver Evans designed an automated flour mill. Eli Whitney, having won the contract to produce 10,000 rifles for the government in 1800, perfected their assembly with interchangeable parts. In 1793, Robert Fulton, an engineer, began designing his paddle steamer, emerging as the *Clermont* in 1807. U.S. industry was steadily developing.

important spinning machinery in his head. Employed by two merchants named William Almy and Moses Brown in Rhode Island, he discarded their old machinery and with the help of a local carpenter who was sworn to secrecy, he started making a Water Frame. In December 1790, production began in the country's first water-driven spinning mill at Pawtucket, Rhode Island.

The factory made a good profit from the start, and Slater soon set up on his

The United States advances

With business taking off in the early nineteenth century, the U.S.A. had to improve its transportation links. The cost of transit was very high and this rose with the building of turnpike roads that charged for travel. Steamboats appeared on rivers, the Great Lakes, and along the coast, assisting trade. Probably the most impressive engineering project at this time was the Erie Canal. It took nine years to build, was 364 miles long, and linked up the Atlantic Ocean with the

The New York and Erie Railroad at Hornellsville, an important junction for travelers to Cleveland or Buffalo. Its owners claimed it was "the most direct route from New York to all Western cities and towns."

Great Lakes. Lowering transportation costs by 90 percent, it provided a massive boost to industry.

Once again, all these projects needed finance. Where did it come from? In 1800, there were only 28 banks in the entire country, but by 1818, the number had risen to 300, with deposits of $160 million in total. The banks and insurance companies encouraged people to save. This, along with profits from agriculture and the successful textile industry, all increased bank deposits. These funds were lent out to entrepreneurs, who invested in factories or civil engineering projects.

U.S. industrialists adopted machines much more quickly than the British did. This was because there was a shortage of skilled labor. Factory owners invested in complex machines that could be operated by unskilled workers. A good example was the sewing machine patented by Elias Howe in 1846. It rapidly created a "ready-made" clothing industry and could be adapted for use in the shoe industry.

The U.S.A. was fortunate in having Pennsylvania—a state rich in iron ore and coal that became the center of the country's heavy industry. The first blast furnace was established by Scottish immigrants, and Andrew Carnegie, also a Scottish immigrant, introduced the Bessemer process for converting iron into steel in 1868.

The shortage of skilled labor in the 1830s and 1840s was overcome by the arrival of European immigrants from countries such as Germany, Sweden, England, Scotland, and Wales. Thousands of people fled the Irish potato famine and emigrated, too.

The U.S.A. rapidly expanded westward during the 1830s at the expense of many Native Americans. Farmers settled the land in very difficult circumstances—it took $600 to establish a farm in Ohio or Indiana. The lack of population and laborers meant that farmers, like factory owners, had to use the latest machinery and cultivation techniques if they were

SOURCE

NEWSPAPER

"…our manifest destiny to overspread the continent allotted [sic] by Providence for the free development of your yearly multiplying millions."

John L. O'Sullivan, editor of the *Democratic Review*, justified the United State' drive west that would lead to the violent confiscation of land from the Native Americans.

John L. O'Sullivan in the *Democratic Review*, July 1845.

to survive. Survive they mostly did. Cities and towns developed. Chicago, fast approaching 100,000 inhabitants in the 1850s, was the center of farm machinery production. Railroad construction tripled during the 1850s. The cities of the "new West"—La Crosse, St. Louis, and Chicago—were all linked by train to the markets of the East Coast. The population rose from 31.4 to 76.2 million between 1860 and 1900. This created a massive demand for goods and the economy boomed.

Despite a divisive civil war between the industrial North and the agricultural South in the 1860s, as the twentieth century approached, the U.S.A. was poised to become the world's industrial leader.

How the railroads powered industrialization

Once the railroad network had been largely completed in Britain, navvies and contractors took their expertise and built railroads all over the world. One of the most successful British contractors was Thomas Brassey, who was responsible for railroad lines in Canada, France, the Crimea (Russia), Australia, Argentina, and India.

The historic moment when the U.S.A.'s east and west coasts were connected by the railroad. Celebrations were held at Promontory Summit, Utah, on May 10, 1869.

The countries that wanted to industrialize understood the importance of railroad building and learned from the British experience. They realized that railroads created a service and a market for the economy. On the service side, railroads were a quicker and cheaper method of transportation than either roads or canals. If costs were low, goods were cheaper and this increased demand. Factory owners and producers saw a railroad link as highly desirable. They could bring in raw materials and dispatch their finished products cheaply. Passenger travel allowed the workforce to be more mobile and flexible.

The construction of a railroad network acted as a huge market for the products of the Industrial Revolution. Vast amounts of iron were required for track, steam locomotives, tools, supplies, and spare parts to keep the railroads running. Iron and timber were needed in large quantities for bridges and the often immense viaducts that were being built. When the boom in German railroad building took place in the 1840s, it gave a great boost to the iron, machine-building, and coal industries.

In the United States, the first transcontinental railroad was completed in 1869, when the United

Pacific Railroad, coming from the west, met the Central Pacific Railroad coming from the east at Promontory Summit in Utah. The directors of both companies hammered in a golden spike on which was written the words *"May God continue the unity of our country as this Railroad unites the two great oceans of the world."* This was a sincere desire in the aftermath of a destructive civil war. Railroads could bring a country closer together, just as the German train network had helped bind together the states of the German confederation. In large countries such as Russia, Canada, and the U.S.A., the railroad could help governments keep control of outlying areas.

Above all, railroads allowed business to develop. In the U.S.A., when the railroad reached the cattle towns of Abilene, Dodge City, and Wichita, Chicago developed the biggest slaughtering and meat-packing industry in the world. Longhorns (a breed of cow) from Texas were driven up the cattle trails for $4 a head. When they reached Chicago by train, they were sold for $40 each.

In all the industrializing nations, the railroad had a huge effect on urbanization. Once railroad lines radiated out from the center of a city, builders bought up land and built streets of houses. Stations serving these suburbs were opened, and workers could commute to jobs in the city centers.

SOURCE

POSTER

The Union Pacific Railroad tried to attract a wide variety of passengers to cross the continent in their trains.

1869. **May 10th.** 1869.
GREAT EVENT
Rail Road from the Atlantic to the Pacific
GRAND OPENING
OF THE
Union Pacific
RAIL ROAD,
PLATTE VALLEY ROUTE.
PASSENGER TRAINS LEAVE
OMAHA
ON THE ARRIVAL OF TRAINS FROM THE EAST.
THROUGH TO SAN FRANCISCO
In less than Four Days, avoiding the Dangers of the Sea!
Travelers for Pleasure, Health or Business
Will find a Trip over The Rocky Mountains Healthy and Pleasant.
LUXURIOUS CARS & EATING HOUSES
ON THE UNION PACIFIC RAIL ROAD.
PULLMAN'S PALACE SLEEPING CARS
RUN WITH ALL THROUGH PASSENGER TRAINS.
GOLD, SILVER AND OTHER MINERS!
Now is the time to seek your Fortune in Nebraska, Wyoming, Arizona, Washington, Dakotah Colorado, Utah, Oregon, Montana, New Mexico, Idaho, Nevada or California.
CONNECTIONS MADE AT
CHEYENNE for DENVER, CENTRAL CITY & SANTA FE
AT OGDEN AND CORINNE FOR HELENA, BOISE CITY, VIRGINIA CITY, SALT LAKE CITY AND ARIZONA
THROUGH TICKETS FOR SALE AT ALL PRINCIPAL RAILROAD OFFICES!
Be Sure they Read via Platte Valley or Omaha
Company's Office 72 La Salle St., opposite City Hall and Court House Square, Chicago.
CHARLES E. NICHOLS, Ticket Agent.
G. P. GILMAN, JOHN P. HART, J. BUDD, W. SNYDER,

Steamships and world trade

With many countries producing more goods in the period after 1840, there was a tenfold increase in the total volume of world trade. This was assisted by the construction of large iron steamers that carried cargoes around the world's numerous shipping lanes.

Although the first steamship to cross the Atlantic was the U.S. steamer *Savannah* in 1819, it ran out of coal before reaching Ireland (sails had to be used to complete the journey). In April 1838, the possibilities of oceangoing steam travel became clear. The civil engineer, Isambard Kingdom Brunel, designed a paddle steamer (powered by steam and paddle wheels), *The Great Western*, which sailed from Bristol, U.K., to the U.S.A. in 15 days and 15 hours. The quickest sailing

ships before this were clippers, which made the fastest crossing in 35 days.

Pad°dle steamer wheels were fragile and could be damaged at sea. In July 1843, Brunel launched the *SS Great Britain*, an all-iron ship that was driven by propellers. In 1845, it crossed the Atlantic in 14 days and 21 hours.

MAP

This is a French map drawn in 1912 showing the main world trade routes. Steamships allowed vast quantities of goods to be traded around the globe.

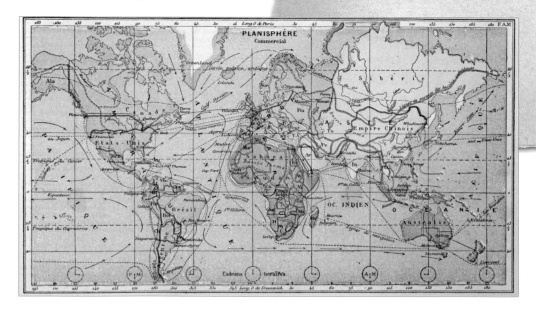

As well as the development of faster steamships, the first Atlantic cable linking Europe and the U.S.A. was completed in 1866 (with the help of another Brunel ship, the *SS Great Eastern*), which also helped in the expansion of trade. In 1869, the Suez Canal was opened, which cut the voyage times between Europe and the Far East. The world was becoming smaller and smaller as travel and communications improved.

Britain became the world's leading sea-trading nation. By 1913, nearly half of the world's steamships were British and one half of all the world's seaborne trade was carried in imported British ships.

At this time, Britain was a great supporter of the idea of "free trade." This was the belief that all nations should be able to trade with each other without taxes known as tariffs. These were taxes on imports coming into a country and made the goods more expensive. Britain disliked tariffs because it felt they restricted and lessened general prosperity. Free trade obviously suited Britain when it was the only industrial power, because it wanted to sell as many goods abroad as possible. The emerging industrial powers, such as Germany and the U.S.A. wanted to protect new industries, so they put tariffs on imports as a defense against British goods.

The world's industrial powers had to constantly search for new customers and markets. They tried to find new markets, for example, in South America, China, and the Far East, where they could sell their goods. Trade could also occur in the other direction. Refrigerator ships carried cheap meat from Australia, New Zealand, and Argentina to Europe. Australia also exported wool, which kept the British and German woolen mills well supplied.

The port of Hamburg was known as Germany's "gateway to the world." It was founded in the twelfth century and became central Europe's most important port in the Industrial Revolution.

Many countries as well as Britain built up empires around the globe. Belgium, France, Portugal, and Germany all had colonies by 1914. The colonies became ready-made markets for the mother country's exports. For example, most Lancashire cotton was exported to clothe the inhabitants of India. This occurred even though India had produced the world's finest cotton yarn and textiles until the eighteenth century.

The importance of cities

One of the most important results of industrialization and population increase was the growth of cities—urbanization. As agriculture modernized, hundreds and thousands of people from the rural areas in Europe could no longer find a livelihood in the countryside. They had to try to find work in the cities instead.

A bird's-eye view of Birmingham, England, in 1860. The city, with the arrival of the canal system, became one of the most important manufacturing centers in the country.

Unsurprisingly, the areas that grew quickest were the settlements with factories. In Britain between 1801 and 1851, Birmingham saw its population rise from 73,000 to 250,000. The population of Liverpool, the port that imported cotton from the U.S.A., increased from 77,000 to 250,000. Manchester in 1772 had 25,000 inhabitants; by 1851, it had 368,000. Similar increases happened in France

and Germany. Moscow in Russia had a population of 400,000 by the late nineteenth century. One by one, countries had more urban than rural dwellers: Britain in 1851, Germany by 1900, and the United States by 1920.

Industrial cities were noisy and dirty. However, there were attractions. They offered jobs, much higher wages than those in the countryside, and stores full of a variety of goods. Cities had colorful markets, entertainment in music halls and theaters, and company to be found in pubs, taverns, bars, and dance halls. The average age of city

SONG

"This Manchester's a fine place,
For trade and other such like movements;
What town can keep up such a race,
As ours has done for prime improvements;

For of late what sights of alterations,
Both streets and buildings changing stations,
Cry bout, 'Laws! Pickle and preserve us!'
Sing hey, sing ho, sing hey down, gaily,
Manchester's improving daily."

Broadside ballad, written between 1830 and 1850.
Quoted in *Nature and Industrialization*, ed Aladair Clayre.

dwellers was lower than that in the countryside. Inhabitants in the cities had an average age of between 20 and 40.

Culturally, the cities were much richer than in the countryside. There were parks, libraries, Mechanics Institutes (offering evening classes), and daily, morning, and evening newspapers. It was the age of exhibitions. The first was in London in 1851; it was called The Great Exhibition and took place in Hyde Park. Paris, France, followed suit in 1855, Philadelphia, PA, in 1876, Chicago, IL, in 1893, and Turin, Italy, in 1896. For many people, the cities were places of opportunity and improvement.

Not only did cities act as magnets for people in the surrounding countryside, but they also attracted migrants from further afield. For example, many people, desperate to better themselves, traveled from other countries to reach Paris or Berlin.

There were similar migrations to other cities. Belgians and Germans helped develop the French towns of Roubaix and Mulhouse. Poles sought work in the heavy industrial center of the Ruhr in Germany. Irish laborers flocked to British cities, especially Liverpool and Glasgow.

The poorest passengers take the air on the SS Pennland, *an emigration ship that sailed the Atlantic from Europe to the U.S.A. in the late nineteenth century.*

Throughout the nineteenth century, the U.S.A. offered great opportunities and was very attractive to European populations. Risking everything on dangerous Atlantic crossings on the notorious "coffin ships" (so called because many died), millions migrated to the U.S.A. looking for a better life.

In the late nineteenth century, the largest city in the U.S.A. was New York. It was the first port of call for immigrants and had a population of more than 1.5 million in 1890. The majority of them were born in Europe: 211,000 from Germany, 190,000 from Ireland, 49,000 from Russia, 48,000 from Austro-Hungary, 40,000 from Italy, and 36,000 from England.

Conditions in the cities

The huge flood of migrants into the industrial towns and cities for work caused overcrowding and placed serious strains on the undeveloped infrastructure. In British cities such as Manchester, it was impossible for builders to keep up with the increase in people. Old houses were crammed full of families who had to live in one room or even share it with another family. The city's basements were notoriously bad to live in. When it rained, they filled up with filthy water.

Any new working-class housing was hastily and poorly built, damp, unhygienic, and lacked ventilation. Under these conditions, diseases spread easily. In 1837, the year Queen Victoria came to the throne in Great Britain, 59,000 people died of the highly infectious lung disease tuberculosis. This disease was common throughout Europe and the U.S.A.

Working-class people were housed in the cheaper districts and had to live among the unpleasant trades that involved the killing and processing of animals for their meat. Workers in slaughterhouses and leather tanneries threw animal waste into drains or streams, or left them to rot. The smells, flies, and filth were shocking. The most serious threat to these crowded cities came from the lack of sanitation. The expanding cities had no proper sewers.

Human sewage was deposited in cesspits (holes in the ground that overflowed with rain water), drains, dumps, streams, and rivers. The sewage infected the drinking water and caused the killer disease cholera. Europe was hit by serious cholera outbreaks in 1831–2, 1848–9, and 1866–7.

As well as disease, fire and crime were constant threats. On October 8, 1871, a fire broke out in Chicago destroying 17,500 buildings and causing $200,000,000 of damage. Three hundred people were killed and 90,000 were left homeless. Crime rates in the industrial cities were high. Many cities had areas that

REPORT

"Punderson's Gardens, Bethnal Green, London. Along the center of the street is an open, sunk gutter, in which filth of every kind is allowed to accumulate and putrefy … in wet weather, the gutter overflows; its contents are poured into neighboring houses …"

Dr. Southwood Smith explained the hazards of east London life in the *4th Report of the Poor Law Commissioners* in 1838.

were dangerous and unsafe. New York had its notorious slum area called "Five Points" and London had St. Giles "Rookery." Both areas were populated by pickpockets, murderers, and illegal gamblers. There were major disturbances by gangs in New York. During 1834–44, there were 200 riots.

During times of unrest in early nineteenth-century Paris, protesters

SOURCE

CARTOON

This is a sketch called *Doing the Slums.* It shows a policeman in the violent Five Points area in New York.

used to block the narrow streets to prevent police and soldiers from entering. In the 1860s, these streets were demolished and replaced by elegant boulevards that were wide enough for troops to march down.

The overcrowded cities contributed to the class divisions of the nineteenth century. The rich fled city centers and

lived separately from the working class. Police forces were introduced by most cities. The London Peelers was formed in 1829. Ordinary people disliked these forces at first because they seemed to be on the side of the rich city dwellers. In time, however, they became familiar and were generally accepted by most.

How things improved

All the countries that went through the transformation from a rural to an urban economy experienced difficult times. There is no doubt that the early years of industrialization caused severe hardship for many people. However, in time, governments did respond to these difficult challenges and progress —albeit slow in many cases—was made.

In Britain, there was major concern about the exploitation of many workers, especially children in the mines and factories. Long campaigns for reform did eventually bear fruit. The Mines Act of 1842 prohibited women and children under ten from working underground. In 1847, after

16 years of campaigning, the Ten Hours Act was passed, which limited women and children under 18 to working 58 hours a week. In 1850 and 1853, this law had to be tightened to

SOURCE

MAP

This map shows Bazalgette's plan for the main sewer lines, which were constructed in 1865 to improve the sewage system of London.

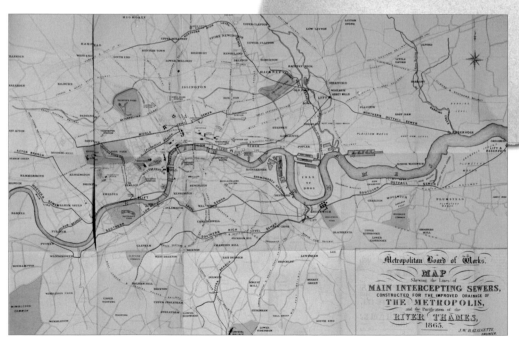

stop shifts going over ten hours. This legislation only protected children in factories. For the thousands of children under ten working in workshops and sweatshops, protection did not come until 1878. These laws were enforced by a few inspectors.

Gradually, cities were cleaned up. After the "big stink" of the summer of 1859, when the River Thames overflowed with human sewage, the government decided to act. Joseph Bazalgette designed and built an impressive 81-mile (130-km) underground sewage system for London that used steam engines pumping clean water to wash the sewage away through glazed pipes. This type of system was applied widely across Europe and the U.S.A. Over time, the birth rate began overtaking the death rate in many European cities.

Parks were created and cities became more pleasant. In Paris, the authorities removed ancient cemeteries and put landscaped parks in their place. Streets were widened and paved and lit by gaslight. They were patrolled by police to make them safer. The unacceptable slum areas in many cities were slowly bought up and cleared. In Britain, the Artisans Dwelling Act empowered local authorities to carry this out.

The idea of vacations developed, ranging from cheap day trips to two-week stays at fashionable resorts. People became more mobile and late

trains ensured that people could visit theaters or music halls and return to the suburbs before midnight.

Schools were set up in all the industrialized countries, and literacy rates rose steadily. With an educated workforce, it was believed that a country would be more industrially competitive. This, in turn, gave rise to daily newspapers, an idea pioneered in the U.S.A. by Joseph Pulitzer and William Randolph Hearst and copied throughout Europe. A new age of communications was dawning when Alexander Graham Bell, a Scotsman, demonstrated his telephone in 1876.

As traffic jams increased, many cities followed London's lead and created an underground railroad system. The Paris Metro, which opened in 1900, has some distinctive station entrances like this one.

Social problems

Although the Industrial Revolution achieved amazing progress in a relatively short space of time, there is no doubt it created winners and losers. In 1900, many European and Americans were better paid, clothed, fed, educated, and had more free time than their grandparents. However, there was a large minority of people who did not share in the developing prosperity.

From its early days, the Industrial Revolution had its casualties and critics. In Britain, skilled manual workers were suspicious of new machines that might put them out of work. In 1811 during the Luddite riots, which took place in Nottinghamshire, rioters attacked the wide stocking frames that produced stockings called "cut-ups" more quickly—but of inferior quality. Popular stories told of a leader named Ned or General Lud, organizing groups of well-disciplined men and leading them to target a particular village and destroy the frames and burn any cut-ups. Inspired by the Luddites, hand-loom weavers in Lancashire and Cheshire attacked the new power looms that were being installed. The government responded by introducing the death penalty as the punishment for machine breaking.

There was a similar leader in the countryside named Captain Swing, who appeared during 1830–1. Farm laborers attacked new threshing machines that

The alleged leader of the Luddites "drawn from life" by an army officer in 1812. Note the burning mill in the background. Rioters blackened their faces or even dressed as women in an effort to conceal their identities.

deprived them of their winter work in the barns threshing by hand. Nineteen of these rioting farm laborers were hanged and hundreds transported to Australia.

The Chartist Movement of the 1830s and 1840s tried to bring working people into the political world with a list of demands called the People's Charter, which included universal suffrage and annual parliaments. The charter failed because it scared off many of the wealthier supporters; the Chartists' energies then went into trade unions, which at first represented only the better-paid and more skilled workers.

The publication in the U.S.A. of Henry George's *Progress and Poverty* (1879) was widely read on both sides of the Atlantic. It questioned why, when nations were becoming richer, the poor seemed to be so numerous. George himself suggested that a tax on land owners might counter inequality.

Workers in the U.S.A. found it difficult to improve their pay and conditions. If trade unionists went on strike, employers responded with lockouts. This meant all employees, even those who were not striking, were stopped from work. They brought in strike-breakers (workers to do the strikers' jobs) and sometimes the army. During a strike at the Pullman Railway Factory in 1894, President Grover Cleveland sent in the troops to call an

SOURCE

REPORT

"Man is the only animal whose desires increase as they are fed; the only animal that is never satisfied."

Henry George (in the picture below) tried to account for the huge division between rich and poor in *Progress and Poverty*, 1879.

end to the strike. The American Railway Union was destroyed. Large unions that were formed for both skilled and unskilled workers, such as the Knights of Labor (1869) and the American Federation of Labor, failed. They suffered from the common view that trade unions were "un-American."

Poverty and the legacy of the Industrial Revolution

By the late nineteenth century, there was a growing unease in Britain and the United States that a significant number of people were living on or below the poverty line. In 1890, Jacob A. Riis published *How the Other Half Lives*, a shocking description of slum life in New York. Charles Booth and Seebohm Rowntree discovered that between a quarter and a third of people living in the British cities York and London lived in severe poverty.

Industrialization brought about the problem of the exploitation of child labor. These boys worked the night shift in a glassworks in Indiana in 1908. Such exploitation still occurs today.

This may have been because nineteenth-century governments had chosen not to involve themselves directly in the affairs of private business, the economy, or social problems unless absolutely necessary. The strength of noninterventionist, or laissez-faire, ideas slowly became less popular. In Germany, the government set up compulsory insurance schemes for worker illness (1883) and accident disability (1884).

In Britain after 1834, a poor person who wanted relief would have to enter a workhouse. Workhouses were deliberately made unpleasant to deter people from applying for help. In practice, they contained the weakest and most vulnerable members of society, such as orphans or the elderly. The new Liberal government that was elected in 1906 tried to do something for the U.K.'s poorest people. The government passed laws that set up Old Age Pensions (1908) and National Insurance schemes for unemployment and sickness (1911).

Obviously the story of the Industrial Revolution does not end here. Industrialization, with its successes and failures, continues today. The high standard of living that the developed world enjoys can be directly traced to the Industrial Revolution. Its legacy has left us with some major challenges: our reliance on unsustainable fossil fuels; overconsumption; pollution of the planet; the lack of fair trade for developing countries, and the dreadful poverty these countries experience.

TIMELINE

1694	The Bank of England is founded.
1709	Abraham Darby uses coke to smelt iron ore instead of charcoal.
1712	Newcomen engine pumps out a coal mine in Birmingham, England.
1733	John Kay's Flying Shuttle weaves cloth more quickly than ever before.
1751	184 Turnpike Trusts established to improve the road network.
1761	Bridgewater Canal opens.
1769	Watt develops his separate condenser, making Newcomen engines more efficient.
1776	Adam Smith's *The Wealth of Nations* is published.
1777	The Grand Trunk Canal, linking the rivers Trent and Mersey, opens.
1779	Crompton's Mule combines all the strengths of the Spinning Jenny and the Water Frame.
	World's first iron bridge spans the River Scvcrn at Coalbrookdale, England.
1781	Watt develops his rotary motion steam engine.
1784	Cort develops puddling and rolling techniques for producing wrought iron.
1787	John Wilkinson builds the world's first iron barge.
1789	Samuel Slater emigrates from England to the United States and transforms the textile industry.

1793	Eli Whitney develops his cotton gin in the United States.
	Robert Fulton begins work on his paddle steamer.
1800	Eli Whitney develops rifle construction with interchangeable parts.
1805	Richard Trevithick's steam locomotive Catch Me Who Can on show in London.
1807	Robert Fulton's paddle steamer *Clermont* operates on the Hudson River, New York.
1825	The Erie Canal opens in the U.S.A.
	The Stockton to Darlington Railway opens with George Stephenson's Locomotion.
1830	The Liverpool to Manchester Railway opens with George and Robert Stephenson's Rocket.
1838	Brunel's steamship the *Great Western* crosses the Atlantic from London to New York.
1840–51	Railway Mania in Britain. 7,000 miles (11,265 km) of track completed by 1851.
1845	Brunel's *SS Great Britain*, the world's first iron ship driven by propellers, crosses the Atlantic.
1863	World's first underground railroad opens in London.
1866	Joseph Bazalgette's underground sewage system in London completed.
1869	U.S.A.'s first transcontinental railroad completed.

GLOSSARY

Apprentice
Someone who is legally bound to an employer while he or she learns a trade.

Aqueduct
A man-made channel carrying water over a river valley.

Assembly
To fit or put something together in an industrial process.

Blast furnace
A very hot area for smelting metals.

Bobbins
Wooden cylinders for winding thread.

Boom
A period of economic prosperity and growth.

Check
A written order to a bank to pay out money.

Civil engineer
An engineer who builds bridges, roads, canals, tunnels, and railroads.

Colliery
Coal mine and the buildings linked to it.

Colony
Country or area ruled by another country.

Commute
To travel some distance from home to a place of work.

Conurbation
A large built-up area consisting of a number of towns that are close together.

Deposits
Amounts of a metal or mineral that has built up naturally in the ground over time.

Domestic system
System of industry that took place at home.

Empire
A geographical area that is owned and controlled by a particular country.

Entrepreneur
A person who organizes business and commercial projects that contain financial risk.

Forge
A workshop that smelts and shapes metal.

Foundry
Building for casting or shaping metal.

Heavy industry
Large-scale industry producing metal and machines.

Infrastructure
The basic foundations of a city, such as roads, sewers, transportation links, and street lighting.

Laissez-faire
From the French "leave be" or "leave alone," the view that governments should not interfere with business.

Locks
A section of a canal with gates at each end letting water in and out. Locks allow barges to go up and down hills.

Loom
A frame for weaving cloth.

Manual
A job or task that is done by hand.

Millwright
A person who designs and builds textile mills.

Packhorse
A horse for carrying goods.

Paddle steamer
A ship that is propelled by paddle wheels at the side or rear of the hull.

Patent
An official document that protects an invention from being copied for a certain amount of time.

Pig iron
Smelted iron used for casting into objects.

Rural
In the countryside.

Sanitation
Keeping buildings and water supplies clean using drainage and the safe disposal of waste.

Seam (coal)
A layer of coal in the ground or in a mine.

Share
An investment of money in a company that entitles the owner to a share in the profits.

Smelt
To heat rock to extract the metal from it.

Sweatshop
A place of work with poor conditions, usually involving long hours and very low pay.

Synthetic dyestuffs
Artificially-made dyes used to color objects.

Threshing
Hitting the ears of wheat to separate the grain.

Trade unions
Organizations of workers. Through its leaders, the union could discuss better pay and conditions with the employer.

Transported
When criminals were sent as punishment to a colony in the U.S.A. or Australia.

Universal suffrage
When every adult can vote.

Urban
To do with a city or town.

Urbanization
The movement of people from rural to urban areas. The growth of towns and cities.

Workhouse
A place where people who could not look after themselves could go to live and work. Workhouses were often strict and unpleasant.

FURTHER INFORMATION AND WEB SITES

FURTHER READING

Smokestacks and Spinning Jennys: Industrial Revolution by Sean Price (Raintree, 2007)

The Industrial Revolution by Sean Connolly (Heinemann Library, 2003)

The Industrial Revolution: A History in Documents by Laura L Frader (Oxford University Press, USA, 2006)

WEB SITES

Due to the changing nature of Internet links, Rosen Publishing has developed an online list of Web Sites related to the subject of this book. This site is regularly updated. Please use this link to access this list: http://www.rosenlinks.com/doc/indu

INDEX

Numbers in **bold** refer to illustrations.

agriculture 4, 6–7
Arkwright, Richard 11

banks 9, **9**, 30
Bazalgette, Joseph 40, 41
Birmingham 36, **36**
Boulton, Matthew 13
Bradshaw, George 25
bridges 9, 17, **17**, 22, 32
Brindley, James 23
Britain 4–25, 35, 36, 37, 38,
  40–41, 42–3, 44
Brunel, Isambard Kingdom 34

canals 13, 23, **23**, 24, 30
Captain Swing 42
charcoal 5, 26
Chartist Movement 43
children 14, 15, 18, **18**, 21, 40,
  41, **44**
cities 28, 31, 33, 36–9, 41, 44
coal 12, 13, 14–15, 17, 23, 32
coal mines 12, 14–15, **15**, 19
Coalbrookdale **16**, 17
coke 16
communications 35, 41
Cort, Henry 16, 17
cotton 8, 35
cotton gin 19, **19**
cotton production 11, 13, 18,
  18, 19, **19**
crime, urban 38, 39
Crompton, Samuel 11
crop rotation 7

Darby, Abraham 15, 16
Davy Lamp 15, **15**
diseases 38
division of labor 18
domestic system 4, **5**
Duke of Bridgewater 23

education 41
empires 8, 35
enclosure, land 6, 7
exhibitions 37
explosions, pit 14, **14**, 15

factory system 18–21
farmers 7, 9, 25, 31
fines 20, 21
fires, urban 38
food 6, 7

France 26, 27, 37, 39, 41
free trade 35
Fulton, Robert 29

George, Henry 43, **43**
Germany 26, 27, **27**, 32, 35, **35**,
  37

housing 38

immigrants 31, 37, **37**
India 8, 35
iron production 5, 13, 15, 16,
  16, 17, **21**, 26, **27**, 31, 32
Ironbridge 9, 17, **17**

Lancashire 18, 19, 42
Liverpool 8, 19, 36
London **9**, 38, 41, 44
Luddites 42, **42**

Manchester 26, 36, 38
McAdam, John 22
meat-packing industry 33
mills 18, **18**, 19, 20, **20**, 21, 29
mining 12, 13, 14, **14**, 15, **15**, 19,
  40
Mule, spinning 11

New York 37, **39**, 44
Newcomen engine 12, **12**, 13

open-field system 6
Owen, Robert 21

paddle steamers **28**, 29, 34
Paris 39, 41, **41**
Pennsylvania 31
pig iron 16, 17
police 39
population growth
  Europe 36
  U.K. 4, 5, 6, 7, **7**
  U.S.A. 28, 31, 36, 37
ports 4, 8, 19, **35**, 36
postal service 23
poverty 39, 44

railroads 24, **24**, 25, **25**, **30**, 31,
  32, **32**, 33, **33**
  underground **41**
reforms 40–41
Reynolds, William **11**

roads 22–3, 30
Russia 27

seed drill **6**, 7
sewage systems 38, **40**, 41
sewing machines 31
shares **8**, 9
Slater, Samuel 28, 29, **29**
slave trade 8
slums 39, **39**, 41, 44
Smith, Adam 18
spinning 5, **5**, 10, 11, 13, **18**, 19,
  20, 21
Spinning Jenny 10, **10**
steam engines 12, **12**, 13, **13**, 19
steamships 28, **28**, 29, 30, 34, 35
Stephenson, George 24

tariffs 35
Telford, Thomas 22
textile industry 4, 5, 10–11,
  18–21, 28–9
tolls 9, 22, **22**
trade 8, 34, 35
trade unions 43
transportation 4, 22–5, 30, 32–5

Union Pacific Railroad 33, **33**
United States (U.S.A.) 19,
  28–31, **32**, 33, 37, **39**, 43, **44**
urbanization 7, 33, 36–9

vacations 41
ventilation, pit 14, 15

Water Frame 11, 29
Watt, James 12, **12**, 13
weaving 5, 19, 29
Whitney, Eli 19, 29
Wilkinson, John 17
women 5, 15, 40
woolen industry 4, 5, 20
workers, factory 18, **18**, 19, **19**,
  20, **20**, 21, 40, 43, **44**
workhouses 44
wrought iron 16, 17